The Dummy's Guide to Boosting Financial IQ

Realistic and Legal Way of Increasing Your Wealth

By: Betty Wright

9781635012774

PUBLISHERS NOTES

Disclaimer – Speedy Publishing LLC

This publication is intended to provide helpful and informative material. It is not intended to diagnose, treat, cure, or prevent any health problem or condition, nor is intended to replace the advice of a physician. No action should be taken solely on the contents of this book. Always consult your physician or qualified health-care professional on any matters regarding your health and before adopting any suggestions in this book or drawing inferences from it.

The author and publisher specifically disclaim all responsibility for any liability, loss or risk, personal or otherwise, which is incurred as a consequence, directly or indirectly, from the use or application of any contents of this book.

Any and all product names referenced within this book are the trademarks of their respective owners. None of these owners have sponsored, authorized, endorsed, or approved this book.

Always read all information provided by the manufacturers' product labels before using their products. The author and publisher are not responsible for claims made by manufacturers.

This book was originally printed before 2014. This is an adapted reprint by Speedy Publishing LLC with newly updated content designed to help readers with much more accurate and timely information and data.

Speedy Publishing LLC

40 E Main Street, Newark, Delaware, 19711

Contact Us: 1-888-248-4521

Website: http://www.speedypublishing.co

REPRINTED Paperback Edition: 9781635012774:

Manufactured in the United States of America

DEDICATION

This book is dedicated to my best friend, Bob. I was inspired by your many business start-and-fail-and-start-again stories. This book should help you become a better money person.

TABLE OF CONTENTS

CHAPTER 1- SETTING THE RIGHT MINDSET TO BOOST YOUR FINANCIAL IQ

True mindset is misconceived, and individuals go through life without properly grasping what that principle is.

One says, "I've an income of so much, and here is my neighbor who has the same; yet yearly he flourishes and I fall short; why is it? I understand all about mindset." He thinks he does, but he doesn't.

There are men who believe that mindset consists in scrimping, in cutting off two cents from the wash bill and doing all sorts of little, mean things. Mindset isn't meanness.

The misfortune is, likewise, that this class of individuals let their mindset apply in only one direction. They fancy they're so wonderfully frugal in saving a penny where they should spend two cents that they think they can afford to waste in other directions.

Before kerosene oil was exposed, one might stop overnight at nearly any farmer's house and get a really good supper, but after supper he may attempt to read in the living room, and would find it impossible with the ineffective light of one candle.

The hostess, seeing his quandary, would state: "it's rather hard to read here evenings; we never have an additional candle except on special occasions." These special occasions happen, perhaps, twice a year. In that way the woman saves 5, 6, or 10 dollars: but the information which may be gained from having the extra light would, naturally, far outweigh a ton of candles.

But the difficulty doesn't end here. Feeling that she is so frugal in candles, she believes she can afford to go often to spend 20 or 30 dollars for ribbons and frills, many of which are not essential. This false belief may frequently be seen in other instances.

You find great businessmen who save old envelopes and scraps of paper. This is all OK; they might in this way save 5 or 10 dollars a year, but being so frugal (only in paper), they believe they can afford to squander time; to have expensive parties, and to drive their fancy cars. This is an illustration of "penny wise and pound foolish." I never knew a man to succeed by applying this sort of mindset.

True sound financial mindset consists in always making the profit exceed the expenditure. Wear the old clothes a bit longer if essential; give up the new pair of gloves; fix the old dress: exist on plainer food if need be; so that, under all conditions, unless some unexpected accident happens, there will be an allowance in favor of the profit.

A penny here and a dollar there saved, continues to accumulate, and in that way the desired result is accomplished. It requires some training, possibly, to achieve this mindset, but when once used to it, you'll discover there's more satisfaction in rational saving than in irrational spending.

Here is a formula which I advocate: I've found it to work a great cure for extravagance, and particularly for mistaken mindset. When you find that you've no surplus money at the end of the year, and yet have a great income, I advise you to take a couple of pieces of paper and mark down each item of expenditure.

Post it daily or weekly in 2 columns, one headed "essentials" or even "comforts", and the other headed "luxuries," and you'll discover that the latter column will be double, or more, larger than the former. The true comforts of life cost but a small portion of what most of us may earn.

Think of the keep up with the Jones' attitude: One may say; "there's a man who has an income of fifty thousand dollars annually, while I have but one thousand dollars; I knew that young man when he was poor like myself; now he's wealthy and thinks he's better than I am; I'll show him that I'm as good as he is; I will go and purchase a fancy car; no, I can't do that, but I'll go and rent one and ride this afternoon on the same road that he does, and therefore prove to him that I'm as good as he is."

My friend, you don't have to do all that; you may easily prove that you are "as good as he is;" you've only to behave as well as he does; but you can't make anybody feel that you're rich as he is. Also, if you act like this, and waste your time and spend your income, you'll remain poor, in order that you might keep up "appearances," and, after all, deceive nobody.

You'll not advance in the world, if your envy forces you into debt. In this country, where we believe the majority ought to rule, we brush aside that principle in reference to style, and let a handful of individuals, calling themselves the aristocracy, run up a fake standard of perfection, and in striving to rise to that standard, we perpetually keep ourselves poor; all the time grinding away for the sake of outside appearances.

How much more sensible to say, "We'll regulate our expenditures by our income, and save something for a rainy day." Individuals should be as sensible on the issue of money as on any other subject. Like actions produce like effects. You can't accumulate a fortune by taking the road that leads to impoverishment. Those who live beyond their means, with no thought of a setback in this life, may never attain monetary independence.

Men and women used to satisfying every impulse, will find it difficult, initially, to cut back their various unnecessary expenses, and will feel it a great denial to live in a littler home than they've been accustomed to, with less expensive furniture, less pricy clothing, less entertainment, and additional extravagances; but, after all, if they'll try saving a "nest-egg," or judiciously investing, they'll be surprised at the joy from perpetually adding to their little "bundle".

The old suit, and the old hat, will work for another season; the water tastes better than champagne; a brisk walk will prove more stimulating than a ride in the finest auto; an evening spent playing a family game will be far more pleasant than a 50 dollar night out, when you begin to know the pleasures of saving.

Thousands of men are kept poor, and tens of thousands are made so after they've acquired riches, in result of living beyond their means. "Easy come, easy go," is an old and true adage. A spirit of pride and vanity, when allowed to have full sway, is the undying problem.

Many individuals, as they set out to prosper, instantly start spending for luxuries, till in a short time their expenses eat up their income, and they become ruined in their absurd attempts to maintain appearances.

CHAPTER 2- DEFINING THE KEY ELEMENTS OF FINANCIAL IQ

Insanity

Naturally, most if not all of us want and crave for something better. It is all part of us if we want a bigger car, a better house, buying good things for the family. We keep hoping for more but, in order to get what you don't have, you have got to do something you have never done before. That simply means: Doing the same thing over and over again YET expecting different results!

As an employee, you can't stay at the same job forever and hope that a miracle will happen and your boss will suddenly give you a raise. You will be lucky that there is no downsizing in your company. Switching to another company will only provide a short term solution to a long term problem. Sure, you can take up a second or even third job, but do you have enough hours and stamina in a day to sustain it? The bottom-line: Trading time for money isn't wise financial sense in the long term. You keep on increasing the hours just to win the rat race, but in the end of the day, you are still a rat on the mill! Increasing your wages only puts you in a higher tax bracket. Your salaries increase but so does your expenses on your house and car.

How will you invest in yourself when all the time you spend working for a company, working for the government paying taxes and working for the bank paying off your house and car? What if you fall sick and can't work tomorrow? Will the government take care of your family? I highly doubt so. So isn't it time you take your finances a tad more seriously?

What is money?

You see, there are many ideas of what people think money is.

Some say it is a form of measurement.

Yes, but a measurement of what? Wealth? In the olden days, people measured wealth by how many cows, sheep and horses they had. But do people measure wealth today by your cows and horses? How about slaves? Was there a time where manpower is considered a hot commodity? Are slaves worth anything today? Are your dollar bills sitting in the bank going to protect you if a recession strikes the country? No, wealth cannot be measured by the dollar bill.

Some say it is a form of power.

Yes, money can give you power, but if you are stuck on a desert island forever with a trillion dollars, will that money mean squat to you? If someone offered you water and a helicopter to fly out of there, you would trade all your money in a split second, so money is not an accurate measurement of power – it heavily depends on how and wisely you use it (hint!).

Many believe it is the root of all evil... and several others take on this belief without much questioning.

Now, now, now... money is NOT the root of all evil (otherwise, why do you think churches still accept monetary donation and charity?). The love of money is the root of all evil. Remember, money is an excellent servant but a terrible master. If you are trading your life away for the dollar, money then has power over your time and life. And unless you have proper financial intelligence, the lack of money can spawn a lot of evil thinking and negative mindset as observed in primarily cheats, thieves, criminals, breakups, freeloaders, cheapskates, and more to name.

But what is money, really?

Money is an idea, backed by confidence.

While money has naturally been developed by merchants in the older days to replace the questionable barter system, money today is literally invented by the rich and wealthy. Entrepreneurs are willing to part with their money to buy other people's time i.e. employees and self-employed people. Employees become their employers' assets because they are used to create more wealth. And here's the thing: as long as you work for money, you are enslaved by it! 80% - 90% of the populations today are being enslaved involuntarily.

What we don't realize is that there is a part of our soul that cannot be bought at whatever price. Would you chop off your little finger if your boss offered you 24 months of your salary immediately? You and I know we are worth more than that. But when you hear of cases of people selling their body parts for cash in some countries, we can have our eyeballs pop out of our eye sockets. On the other hand, we occasionally DO sell out a part of ourselves for money like a donkey and a carrot.

Awareness before Change

Now don't get me wrong: I'm not banging on working at a job (I worked at one before I became an Internet Entrepreneur). But let's face it: our needs today are growing more than ever before in any period of history. Prices go up, salaries don't. There are more baby boomers than ever and have very little pension to show for their decades of years of work efforts. And there is no guessing to how many people really, really hate the unhealthy, hectic lifestyle of getting up early, coping with stress for most parts of the day, join traffic jams, spend more money and time in traveling, enjoy very little rest, and repeat the viscous cycle.

Definitely doesn't paint a nice financial and lifestyle picture, huh?

The first step to change is to be aware of the problem. Awareness before change (or ABC for short) is necessary if you are to make any changes in life to start taking control of your financial life and then get out of the rat race. We need the awareness to know what state we are in so we know where we are going. For starters, indulge me in a quick exercise as we exit this chapter shortly:

Time and Money

There are generally 4 types of people in the world:

(1) No time, and no money.

Most employees fall into the category. You can't go shopping on a Tuesday afternoon or fire your boss whenever you like. Most employees can't even save money in their pension to last 3 years!

(2) No time, lots of money.

Self-employed, professionals and small business owners are in this category. They are slightly better off than the employee because they earn more, but they have to work even harder than employees to keep up with the diminishing profit margins, competition and servicing their customers.

(3) Got time, no money.

A lot of farmers, villagers, college dropouts or bums have lots of time but no money. Maybe ignorance is bliss, but without a stable source of income, how long can you last many days forward?

(4) Got time, and lots of money.

It is the category that big business owners, landlords, investors are in. Imagine, not having to work for money, but having money to work for you by investing them and earning profits by using your money to make money.

CHAPTER 3- CREATING A MAP TO SUCCESS

Inside you there's a hungering for more. Is it meaning, contact or a richer understanding of life? No one has ever acquainted such individuals with the concept of perpetual possibility. "As a man thinketh, so is he." A major mode to manifesting the life you wish is to think over what you wish out of life. What is it that you wish to do with your life? A great exercise is to take a sheet of paper and put down the answers to the accompanying questions:

- What is my deepest want?
- What would I like to achieve in my lifetime?
- What would I like to achieve this year?
- Where would I wish to be in five years?
- Where would I wish to be in twenty years?
- What am I great at?

Check into all fields of your life:

- Your line of work
- Your relationships
- Your wellness
- Your financial state of affairs
- How you have fun (how you spend your vacations)

After you've put down a list of what you wish to achieve in your life, you'll need to set priorities for them. Simply take the list that you put down and provide every topic 1 - 5 points; whereas 1 is the least crucial and 5 the most. Now you've priorities in your life, which will help you determine where you wish your attention to be. It's an easy equation: comprehend simply that you wish to spend most of your time with the number 1 matter on your list. Spend somewhat less time with the number 2 entry on your list – and so forth for numbers 3 through 5.

There's no need to slice the day into time slots. Just by doing this exercise you're programming your consciousness to spend time harmonizing with your list.

Let's presume you'd like to discover your life partner in the next 2 years, and that this is your chief goal, at the very top of your list. When you check into your thought process at the end of the day and you discover that you've not spent most of your spare time addressing this goal, you've a misalignment, and you might never accomplish your goal. When this occurs merely realize it and correct accordingly.

Working all day only to sit down on your couch and watch television won't get you where you wish to be. You have to take action to manifest your goal(s), for instance:

- Take action by signing on for a class
- Enroll in a weekend seminar on a matter that fascinates you
- Go to a workshop that centers on your interest
- Spend time at places where you are able to meet individuals

If your goal happens to be that you wish to be a millionaire inside 5 years, and you're spending only 5 minutes of your time every day to achieve this goal, then don't be surprised if your financial state of affairs never alters.

There's another crucial aspect of manifestation here that calls for consistency. Let's presume you've made your priority list and everything on your list feels great up to now. It's really crucial that you're in emotional concord with your goals – they have to feel correct to you. If you merely make goals in your mind that are not useful to you then you'll discover yourself having a difficult time working to accomplish them.

What occurs with most individuals scenario is that they've a goal that feels correct for them, then they begin working at their goal. Put differently, they place their attention into making their goal a fact. A couple of weeks go by and nothing occurs. Now dismay kicks in and the goal for some reason appears unreachable, the motivation is down to zilch.

This is the point where you have to feel your dismay. Don't simply place it away or discount it – face it as totally and consciously as you are able to. This may be unpleasant for you however it will help you get nearer to your goal. How is this? When you wish to alter your reality you evidently have to do something differently than what you've done previously.

So this is where the truth check comes in. You look around and can't see any change.

But changes might have already happened in your thinking and conduct. You might have set matters in motion that you can't yet see. Dismay sets in when you presume that matters ought to be happening sooner than you're ready for them. Remember – there are no unrealistic goals, only unrealistic time frames.

So feel your dismay and let it resolve. View what you've done and realign your strategies. If one way doesn't lead to success don't quit at that point – merely attempt another. If you stick with a goal you'll accomplish it.

Occasionally you might push too hard when you simply have to let go and take the pressure off. You question yourself at this point, trusting there's nothing you are able to achieve. Go to the place in your brain where you know you can't bomb. Reading a book or viewing a motivational movie might help to get you realigned with your mighty source.

You Are Capable of Amassing Wealth Regardless of Your Status

Each of us is unparalleled, having particular talents and gifts. It's something innately built-in in all of us, a compounding of energy patterns leading toward a natural kinship for particular issues in life, particular ways of being. Among the most crucial jobs in your life is to discover these talents and gifts inside yourself, which is an acknowledgement of what you've brought into your creation.

Let's presume that you're presented a hammer without having any cognition of how to use this tool. Remain with me now – this is a stark over-simplification of a highly crucial aspect of your truth. You're presented nails but you utilize the incorrect end of the hammer. You can't see any success with achieving your task of beating in the nails. You've the tool but not the cognition of its correct use. Likewise, how may we manage our lives without understanding the many tools usable and their applications? You may even have an instant of enlightened clarity. We may all relate to at last understanding something that had been messing us up. Wouldn't it be nice if somebody had shared the essential info in advance – before going through frustration and maybe surrender?

Realizing your own strengths and talents is utterly crucial for any further steps you take in life. Putting them down ought to make them more real to you if you're not used to thinking of them. If you understand your distinctive strengths and gifts you ought to be able to write them down in a couple of sentences without having to think too much about the procedure. If you're not certain, or you truly have no clue, here are a couple hints that will help you describe them:

Remember your childhood:

• What were the playthings you liked to play with?
• What were you intrigued with?
• What did you like most to play?
• What gifts did you want to get for your birthday and Christmas?
• What did you aspire to become in your future?

Ask your nearest acquaintances:

Tell your acquaintances that you wish to reassess your talents and you need a realistic opinion from them. Make certain to ask your acquaintances to be 100% truthful with you. Let them take a new look at you and ask them to blank out what you're doing professionally – keep it on a personal plane.

• What do your acquaintances believe you're good at?
• What do they believe your talents are?
• What do they urge you ought to do with your life?

Ask yourself a couple of questions

Take a notebook and read through these enquiries. Make certain you open your mind and let these questions solidify in your imagination. Don't take these queries too earnestly, play with them and likewise put down what bobs up spontaneously – these are occasionally the most fundamental answers.

These questions are configured to bring your consciousness out of the normal mentality. The most dependable solutions are always discovered outside the normal domain of thinking. Remember, your mind is part of the collective awareness; consequently you've access to all info. Your mind is connected to the infinite source of all cosmos.

What would you do if you possessed enough income not to work ever again?

• What were your ambitions when you were younger?
• What do you believe is impossible for you to accomplish?
• What would you do if you acquired 5 million dollars?
• What would you do if this was the crack of doom?
• What would you do if you could not bomb?
• What are your specialties and talents?
• Do you have a want but don't know how to satisfy it?
• What do you like most about other people?
• What would your ideal life-style look like?
• What does success mean for you?
• What makes you truly happy?
• What does a perfect day look like for you?
• What would you do if there were no limitations?
• What would you be esteemed and recognized for?
• Where do you view your life in 10 years?
• If you were immortal, what would you accomplish with your life?

- What needs to shift to make this a better Earth?
- What are you proud of?
- What would you like to achieve this year?
- What would you do differently if you could begin once again?

Discovering your strengths and talents is like first constructing the basement for your home. It's your foundation. It's like the dirt from which a solid and beautiful tree may grow. It supplies you with your unique potential. It's the unique endowment that came with you when you were born. You are being asked here to nurture it till it's substantial enough to guide you in your life.

Don't blow your time chasing somebody else's ambition or goal or anything that isn't given to you that you can't claim 1st as your own. Utilize the gifts you came in with or the ones you acquired along the way. You might become really good at something but you'll never discover true, lasting happiness with it if you can't own it totally.

Utilize whatever tools you feel comfy with. Attempt to discover a way to dig deeper into yourself. This is your life – and you're worth it!

If good health is the cornerstone of success and happiness in life, how crucial it is that we ought to study the laws of wellness! And yet how many individuals there are who pay no attention to this, but absolutely breach it, even against their own innate inclination. We should know that the "ignorance" is never bliss. A youngster might poke its finger into the fire without knowing it will burn, and so suffers.

Many individuals knowingly violate the laws of nature against their better impulses, for the sake of style. For example, there's one thing that no one would ever naturally love, and that's tobacco; yet how many individuals there are who purposely train an unnatural appetite, and get to love it.

They have got hold of a poison; or rather it takes a firm hold of them. A perilous feature is that this artificial appetite, like jealousy, "develops by what it feeds upon;" when you love that which is unnatural, a heavier appetite is produced for the injurious thing than the natural desire for what is harmless. There's an old proverb which states that "habit is second nature," but an artificial habit is firmer than nature.

Youth regrets that they're not grown; they would like to go to bed children and wake up adults; and to accomplish this they copy the foul habits of their elders. Little Mike sees his father or uncles smoke a pipe, and they say, "If I could only do that, I would be a grownup too; uncle John has left and left his pipe of tobacco, let me try it." He acquires a match and lights it, and then puff away. "I'll learn to smoke; but it tastes bitter; he thinks" later he grows pale, but he persists, sticks to it and perseveres till finally he conquers his natural appetite and becomes the victim of acquired tastes.

His palate has become narcotized by the harmful smoke. This shows what expensive, useless and harmful habits men will get into. I speak from experience. I've smoked till I trembled, the blood rushed to my head, and I had a quivering of the heart which I thought was a heart condition. When I consulted my doctor, he said "stop using tobacco." I wasn't only injuring my health and spending a lot of money, but I was setting a bad example. I obeyed his advice.

These comments apply with tenfold force to the utilization of intoxicating drinks. To make revenue, calls for a clear brain. A man has got to see that 2 and 2 make 4; he has to set all his plans with contemplation and caution, and closely examine all the details and the ins and outs of business.

As no man may succeed in business unless he has a mind to enable him to set his plans, and reason to lead him in their execution, so, regardless how plentifully a man might be blessed with intelligence, if the mind is muddled, and his judgment distorted by intoxicating drinks, it's impossible for him to conduct business successfully.

How many great opportunities have passed, never to come back, while a man was sipping a "social glass," with his acquaintance! How many dopey bargains have been made under the influence, which temporarily makes its victim believe he's rich?

How many crucial chances have been postponed till tomorrow, and then eternally, as the wine has thrown the system into a state of lethargy, neutralizing the energies so crucial to success in business?

What's Keeping You from Achieving Your Goals?

Are these familiar to you?

- They're just more prosperous than I am
- They've better training than I do
- They were born into a wealthy family
- They're white and have more beneficial opportunities than I do
- They already had the revenue to begin a business
- They already had the revenue to invest in realty
- They're brighter than I am
- They're younger than I am
- They look better than I do
- They likely work harder than I do

The list likely carries on filling many pages. Money is the topic that renders the most notions, followed by the issue of relationships.

You might not understand this yet, but your notions are the pattern for your reality. If you knew that, would you designedly create one from the list above? Likely not, as these notions are not supportive at all. These beliefs produce a truth that leaves you 'playing' the dupe, and moreover, keeps you right where you are. You're not bettering your life one bit. Why are we producing these notions in the first place, when we understand that they're not constructive in the least?

The answer dwells nature of our consciousness. Most of us were told that there's a universe out there and this universe conditions our truth. It's the common notion that life happens to us. Most of us get these notions supported several times per day. The consequence is that our consciousness becomes imprinted every day with the same message.

In the meantime, as grownups, we're not even cognizant that our life, 'as it happens' is constructed around a notion. It becomes a fundamental reality that we prove to ourselves in every moment.

So how do we get out of this quandary? We have to take a step backwards and view our notions. Take a sheet of paper and a pencil and put down all the notions you have about income. Don't think excessively, be spontaneous. When you've run out of your own notions, consider what others notions are about money.

Then mark each notion with an 'I' or an 'S' depending if the notion is hindering or supportive. Hindering notions don't support producing wealth, supportive notions do. Now, view your list and count every supportive and hindering notion. What is your score?

How many hindering notions do you have, and how many supportive notions do you have?

Recognize that all the hindering notions don't support the production of fortune. Now, take a fresh sheet of paper, and brainstorm notions that will precisely produce the wealth you'd like to have. When you're done with the list, check out each of your fresh notions and produce a mental picture. Hold this image for at least ten - twenty seconds. You might require some practice, but each time you do it, you'll get better at it. Do this exercise in a calm, tranquil and relaxed environment, as this will help to impress these notions into your consciousness.

Remember, notions are the design of what will manifest in your life. With a little preparation, you'll be able to move onto the next stage, which is feeling your notions. Feel as though these fresh notions, that foster what you truly want to create, have really been manifested.

- How does it feel to be a millionaire?
- How does it feel to have copiousness in your life?
- How does it feel to have more income than you are able to spend?
- How does it feel to give to other people?
- How does it feel to purchase something without having to view the price?

Whenever you see yourself thinking or speaking a hindering belief about money, quit what you're doing. Return to the place in your mind where you call up one of your purposely created beliefs about revenue, and connect with it. The more you accomplish this, the more you'll train your brain to think in a fresh way, a way that heads to living an abundant and favorable life.

CHAPTER 4- HOW TO ACQUIRE WEALTH – THE LEGAL WAY

Everyone wants to make more money, but people are generally split into two categories:

Those who bring results after they are promised wealth first

Or

Those who bring the results first, then are rewarded by others afterwards

Let's explore the two groups in depth.

Those who only move their butts after promised big fat paychecks are more like employees, freshmen, or mercenaries. There is no right or no wrong with this kind of thinking, but consider: you are once again, trading your precious time for money. Instead of investing your time in an ASSET that generates money, you spend your time working on something that is short term, limited wealth, and does not give you income long after you have stopped working. Consider also, that this kind of short term vision will only produce limited or temporary results at best. Ever seen a security guard asleep at work when the boss is not around? Furthermore, the part where our emotions get the better of us is when we allow our lives to be run by chasing the dollar. It is evident whenever an employee is offered a higher salary, more medical benefits and longer vacations that their heart starts pumping faster.

A higher salary doesn't mean less financial problems. On the contrary when your income goes up, your commitments, your tax bracket and your time spent in your company increases. The greater your salary, the weaker your position because if your boss is paying you a 5 figure income and calls for an emergency meeting, you had better rush over to the office even if you are halfway making love to your wife! I think the best definition of an employee/boss relationship can be summed up as this. An employee will only do the bare minimum to keep the boss from firing them and a boss will only pay the bare minimum to keep an employee from leaving.

Now let's explore the other group. There are many creative people, inventors, entrepreneurs, and business leaders who fall into this category. An entrepreneur is someone who always has good ideas.

The first obstacle we need to overcome if we want to succeed in the second group is to stop working for money. What does this mean? Isn't making money part and parcel of having good financial IQ? What I mean by 'stop working for money' is not working for free. Rather, it means work so as to gain the necessary skills you need to be a successful entrepreneur (or inventor, investor). Allow me to illustrate: If you lack the contacts for running a business, where would the best place be to look for contacts? Of course, at your competitor's. How about product knowledge? Then work with a company that will teach you all the ins and outs of the tricks of the trade. Not familiar with the production line of a factory? Work in one! Learn the ropes or manage the factory workers. Fear of talking to people? Get a sales job where you will be forced to talk to lots of people. It is also a great way to develop perseverance! Don't you know that the best education you can get is in real life! Not at a lecture hall.

The bottom-line is: not everybody has what it takes to succeed as an entrepreneur! It is not that easy. Many lack the perseverance, the creative mindset, the financial capabilities or the necessary people to get the job done and usually give up too early before any results can be seen! The fastest way to apply those skills and succeed is to learn hands on and you even get paid in the process! Don't get absorbed with how much you are paid.

When Donald Trump was selecting candidates in The Apprentice, their first task was to go to the streets and sell lemonade! Many would find it a degrading task. But to The Donald, it was very important: If you can't even do something as simple as sell lemonade, how on earth can you handle a daunting task like running the Trump Empire? Again, let me emphasize: Would you trade time for short term money? (Money stops coming in when you stop) Or Trade time and money for a long term asset that generates you income? (Even long after you have stopped) God created us with a brain. All we need to do is look around us and observe problems to overcome because every problem is an opportunity in disguise. It is all up to you. You may or may not see the results in the short term, but by using our brains and the resources around us, we can create true value that others are willing to pay for what we have to offer.

3 Ways of Making Money

Let me summarize the 3 Ways of Making Money

- Trading Time for Money - employees, self-employed
- Manifesting & Using Creative Ideas - inventors, artists, programmers
- Leveraging on resources and other people - business people, leaders

If you are a professional, have you ever explored writing an e-book about your field of expertise? If well written, it could provide a new income stream, instead of you selling out your time serving your clients. How about a computer programmer? You can come out with your own revolutionary product instead of selling your ideas to the company you work for. How about real estate, instead of selling houses, you can pool financial sources to buy houses cheap, increase their value and sell them off at a higher price. It just takes a little time and research to find good ideas. Is money a problem? Seek out loans if you can take the risk. Pool money from many investors or seek a grant. The sky is the limit when it comes to making money. Again, which way do you want to achieve wealth? Answer: it's totally up to you

The 4 Fundamentals to Your Future Empire

When you are looking at building yourself financially, there are a few things that you must make sure you have with you. These are your allies in your quest for financial empowerment – they are your four fundamentals – without which you will find this journey very difficult. Here we take at a look at these four essentials in brief and throughout this eBook, we shall take a detailed look at what they really mean.

Assets

Assets are what you utilize in order to start empowering yourself financially. These assets include monetary as well as monetary resources. Most people only consider monetary assets when they speak about assets. They consider things like their bank balance, their property, their cars, their stocks, etc. as assets. However, there is much more to assets than just these materialistic things.

Here we take a look at assets other than the usual material ones.

- Goodwill

Your good name in the market is a veritable asset. It could be your name or the name of your company, your brand, etc. Whatever goodwill your name has accumulated, you could certainly use it in improving your profits, and hence it becomes an asset. For instance, if you launch a new product with the same name of your previous successful product, it already gets a lot of foundation to succeed. That's the reason big name companies sell their goodwill when they give out franchises.

- Your Qualifications, Eligibilities and Experiences

Everything that you do in your life is an asset in itself. These are things you can tap on in order to empower yourself in a better manner. For example, if you are a postgraduate, you could use that qualification to pitch in for financing a research plant you want to set up. If you have worked in a particular area, your chances of earning in that area are more.

- Your Family, Friends and Other People

Everyone that you come in contact with is a potential asset for you. You are what your family makes you, and that decides your capabilities to a large extent. Also, your friends make you and so do other people that you come in contact with. People are so important to businesses today that there are complete business models that are set up on this concept. Take network marketing, for instance, better known as MLM, where people directly tap into the people they know in order to enhance their income capabilities.

- How to Build Your Assets

Being financially empowered means you have to have enough money so that you don't lack for funds when you need them. You have to be rich enough to have money to cover all your needs and desires. The desires part needs to be seen with more careful attention here, because most people have adequate money to cover their needs. It is when they need to realize one of their dreams that they feel they are lacking in proper funds.

It is necessary that you have the right kind of financial empowerment to chase your goals and intentions. This is where asset building becomes important in your route to financial empowerment. In this context, you try to build on what you can call your own so that you can build more to call your own.

There are various ways in which you can begin focusing on asset building.

- Proper Investments

Investing is the best route to building assets. Find ways to make investments, such as in fixed deposits in banks, money-back insurance policies, stocks or whatever suits your interests. The channel you select for investment should be safe and should guarantee you high returns.

- Sniffing Out Opportunities

Opportunities are all around us, but we don't know how to get at them. Keep your eyes wide open. If there is a business venture that interests you, learn more about it till you know all that there is to it. There are several high-paying opportunities like network marketing that can pay you back a lot without requiring much investment. Keep your mind receptive to such opportunities.

- Involve Your Friends and Family

Most of us shut out our near and dear ones when it comes to asset building. We have to understand that assets are not just monetary. There are various other things that can help us build ourselves financially, and toward this end, we have to realize that the role of the people in our lives is quite significant.

Education

Education is veritable factors in empowering yourself financially because your career is going to depend on how educated you are. However, education does not just mean academic qualifications — everything that you do in the pursuit of achieving something counts toward your education. Even reading a manual to understand how a particular software application operates will be education for you because you can use it in future in some or the other way to enrich what you have got.

- Why You Should Invest In Education

What we don't really realize is that our tryst with financial empowerment begins much sooner than we think. It isn't when we are 20 and thinking about a career; it is right when we are 3 and attend our first school. In fact, our financial empowerment begins even before that when our parents lovingly and patiently tell us what is what. All those questions, all those attempts at gathering information and, later, education, are nothing but steps toward financially empowering ourselves.

For, what is education if not a way to empower ourselves in every way, including financially?

A lot of people tap into their educational qualifications when they are looking for a job, pitching for a promotion, applying for a freelancing assignment or even when applying for financial assistance for a commercial venture. The educational qualification is a kind of abstract collateral; it is something people judge your financial worth with. If you are better qualified they know that you will keep sailing through and hence they don't mind extending a better financial help for your ventures. They don't mind investing in your ventures either because they consider you as a worthy candidate with their money.

That is the reason, it is important to learn as much as possible. After becoming the President of the United States, one of the first things Barack Obama did was to give a clarion call to his people to „go back to school". This does not really mean physically going back to school, but it means continuing to learn something or the other as we did when we were younger.

Come to think of it, when we were at school, we would learn a new thing each day. Are we doing that right now? At school, we enriched our minds each day and became what we are today. But why has this process of „becoming" stopped for some people? Why do some people think that their learning age has ceased? We need to educate ourselves continuously, till the last day of our lives and keep improving ourselves.

When we are more educated, we not only learn better avenues to earn money but we also learn how to manage the money properly so that it keeps growing. No form of education should be intimidating and there is no age when you cannot begin learning something.

Investment

Investing is an asset because this helps you in securing money for the long run. When things are going the way they shouldn't, your investments matter a lot. Even when everything is hunky-dory, your investments build up your financial portfolio like few other things can.

Recreation

You might not willingly take this as a factor for financial empowerment, but the fact is that you need to enrich your mind in order to stay healthier and hence make yourself more stable monetarily. Some forms of recreation can actually directly help in improving your economic standing as well.

The common mentality of most people is that when they are getting some recreation for themselves – in whatever form that might be – they are actually wasting time. They think that by giving themselves some amusement, they are actually depriving themselves of the opportunity of being able to earn something. Proverbs like "Wasting time is akin to wasting money" don't help matters one bit. But we should remember that "All work and no play make Jack a dull boy." But, is it only a dull boy that Jack can turn out to be? No, worse things can happen if you deprive yourself from proper routes of recreation.

You have to understand what recreation means first. To recreate means to free up your mind and utilize it in doing something that you really like to do. It means to unwind yourself from your daily rigmarole of work. Since our mind is not a machine, but a living organ with blood and tissues in it, it does need this kind of unwinding ourselves.

But there is a subtle point that you must understand. Every person chooses his or her form of recreation and this is most times connected with what they do professionally. For example, for a person who teaches, reading could be a form of recreation. Now, this is actually helping their profession in various ways. This person is able to expand his or her knowledge and that really helps them in their profession. For a professional sportsperson, looking at someone else's game could be recreation. Now, they could pick up various tips from that and learn.

However, even when you think there are no obvious benefits of your form of recreation on your profession, there are actually several benefits. Consider that you have a desk job. Your mode of recreation is to shoot villains in computer games. How does this help your profession? It actually does, in a very poignant way, because it helps clear the clutter of monotony that your job has created and gives you a chance to do something that revitalizes your energy. You are refreshed and can even return to work the next day in a better mood.

Remember that empowering yourself financially does not mean immersing yourself in money-related thoughts and keeping yourself there all the time. Sometimes, you have to come out of those shackles and think in a liberated manner. This helps you rethink things and you begin looking at the world with a renewed perspective.

The Sum of Five: A Key Aspect in Financial Empowerment

The Sum of Five is a key aspect in financial empowerment. It is a rule, a rule which you apply in order to keeping yourself dynamic. It ensures that you don't remain stuck in the rut when you have achieved a modicum of success, but you keep improving upon it and keep moving northward.

So, what does the Sum of Five state?

The Sum of Five states that if your income is the sum total of the five people closest to you. If the five most prominent people you are dealing with financially make less money than you do, then it is time for you to find some more financial collaborators.

This is the statement of the Sum of Five, but you need not judge it by what it actually says. Look at what it means. What it means is this – When you are involved in business collaboration with several people, you must take a look at how much the five people closest to you are earning. Here, we don't really mean a number at all. The „five" is irrelevant. You have to look at the people you are dealing with at all times. If the people you are dealing with are making more money than you are, you must continue your efforts till you reach their level. But if they are all making less money than you, it means you have reached a point of stagnancy and now you need to find more people to hobnob with.

You won't be mistaken if you find this law to be a bit selfish. Actually, it isn't that way. We all believe and accept that change is imminent. We say that all the time. Then why do we not change the circumstances that surround us? We tend to live in the same situation for life, without trying to think we should take higher leaps. This is where we make the absolute error.

If we want to progress, it is important for us to improve the situation that we are surrounded with. It is important for us to change the set of people we regularly deal with. There is a saying in an Indian language that says, "A man doesn't really succeed in life unless he leaves his childhood behind." What it really means is that we should not cling to our past more than we should. In life, we continue climbing the rungs of ladder of success but since we tend to think we have reached our zenith, we never continue moving upward. This is when the downward fall begins.

CHAPTER 5- PEOPLE'S TAKE ON INVESTING

What comes in to your mind when you mention the word investing? Does it mean, putting your money in insurance, mutual funds, the stock market or even high-yield investments? Other people might only think about investing when they are about to die and they haven't left anything for their offspring. Some even shiver when they hear the word, often claiming that they have no money to invest or feel that is too complicated a subject to even discuss about. Many people even invest heavily in health supplements, personal trainers and beauticians to live longer, healthier or even look younger! Imagine the advertising budget for beauty companies nowadays. All these are legitimate concerns when it comes to investing, but I am talking about the most important investment a person can make in his lifetime.

The Most Important Rule in Investing

The most important and No.1 rule is "Invest in Yourself" – if you don't, who else will?

Your parents will only invest in your education only until you leave college. But that is just the basic necessities provided and does not teach you important lessons about financial education. Would you depend on colleges or universities to teach you how to make money? Most colleges only teach you skills so you can earn money working for other people. How about business school? Honestly, if business lecturers are such experts at business, why are they still lecturing there instead of making a fortune in business ventures? Would your boss teach you how to succeed in business so that one day, you will be in his position?

You and only you have to be proactive enough to take that responsibility

You see, when you invest in yourself, it means taking on the importance of educating yourself. Education not in the academic or technical sense, though they are necessary skills to be developed in life. Our education doesn't stop at college. For most working adults, their education enters retardation stage after they leave college. They stop learning and therefore they stop growing. They only grow sideways from eating too much pizzas or take-out during their busy lunch breaks.

We know that IQ is important right? But why aren't the most intelligent people in the world the richest people in the world? There are many accountants and financial planners rushing to their cars every evening trying to beat the after work traffic congestions! They are not rich!

How about EQ or Emotional quotient? Do working hard, having a great attitude and a positive mindset solve our financial situation?

These are important when running a business, but let me illustrate: If you are driving from Boston to New York using the wrong road map, you won't get to our destination no matter how fast you drive your car (working hard)! You can work harder, but you would only get to the wrong destination faster! You may have the best attitude in the world or the most positive mindset, but you still won't get to New York (although the journey wouldn't bother you since you are feeling positive about it).

Understanding the Importance of Financial Education

You must FIRST invest in your Financial IQ.

Having good financial IQ is not about saving tons of money or dumping them into mutual funds. It is developing healthy relationship money and building a wealth of assets that will generate you money. What does it take to develop your financial IQ?

Delayed gratification is one of the most important aspects to developing your financial IQ. Take this as a hypothetical example. Would you pay for a pint of milk or a cow?

If you buy milk, it is consumed and it is over. You will have to buy milk over and over again when it is finished. Even if the milk costs less than a cow, in the long run, you will still be buying milk again and again. Now, if a cow were to cost 50 times more than milk, you might pay through your nose when you purchase the cow, but after consuming 50 pints worth of milk from the cow, you would break even on your investment and save more money in the future. In fact, the cow might give birth to 2 or more calves and you could sell one of them for profit! Get the idea? EVERYONE is capable of creating wealth. When you take a beat up old car and give it an overhaul, paint it with a new coat of paint, and change a few more parts to make it start running again, you could sell that car for more money than if it was just a beat up old car. You would have created wealth in the process! How about a farm? If you turn a farm into a country home getaway resort, wouldn't the value of the farm land increase manifold?

It is the same principle for chefs, computer programmers and craftsmen. The sum of the whole is greater than the parts. We are all capable of creating wealth even out of thin air and that is the first step to getting our creative juices flowing. The value of anything is defined by supply and demand. You don't need to be a Major in economics to understand this. Money is just an idea. Remember the desert island example? The true measurement of money is not the cents or dollars it represents. If you have developed a product that people want, would they pay more to you than usual? Would you apply your skills in creating good assets?

Bottom-line is this:

Invest in assets that bring long term value. Anything that brings you more income is an asset. Don't invest too much in liabilities like cars or boats. Even houses are not considered assets until they are fully paid off (If you lost your job tomorrow and you can't pay for your house, is your house an asset or liability?) Are you willing to step out of your comfort zone and pay the price for financial IQ or ignore the signs of the times and expect your boss, the government and the bank to take care of you financially for the rest of your life, living below your means and never taking risks to better your family's future?

How to Keep Moving Forward

Our finishing touch will be to speak about how you must remain always moving toward the top. In fact, we have alluded to this already when we spoke about the Sum of Five. When you try to equate yourself with your collaborators and then find better collaborators if you find they are all doing much worse than you, you are staying upwardly mobile. When you mix around with people who have a particular kind of status, it automatically begins rubbing on you. Consciously or subconsciously, you begin taking steps to be with them, and sooner than you think, you are there. You get that one important breakthrough and you get to be with these people.

If you have used the four fundamentals in the right way, and are still constantly using them, then you will keep shaping yourself to be a more significant person financially. You will be going upward all the time and this is what really matters.

One thing that you have to keep in mind is that you must broaden your approaches. Once you are set with something, move on to other things. We have spoken about how you must be always aware of opportunities and take them in your stride. Learn how to make the most of them.

Think positive. Think big. When you do that, you usually do big. If you confine yourself to thinking narrow-mindedly, you are going to stay there. A lot of modern philosophers have laid great emphasis on the importance of thought – Stephen Covey, Rhonda Byrne, and Paulo Coelho – and you have to understand that there is great truth in this. When you think positively about something, things automatically energize themselves to make that happen. You know this fact in another form already probably – the Law of Attraction. Yes, this law can help you greatly in financially empowering yourself. Get acquainted with it today.

CHAPTER 6- TIPS TO SUCCESSFULLY GET OUT OF ANY FINANCIAL MESS

There are two methods I can recommend about getting out of a financial mess.

Defensive Strategies

The first one is defensive:

Cut down what you are already spending on. You can't start a business being in a financial mess. Cash Flow is more important than revenue. And you need to have lots of cash flow coming from your pockets if you are going to succeed.

Here are some things you can cut down on

- Smoking – if you can't quit, just cut down on a few sticks
- Alcohol – booze can drain your finances faster than a running tap
- Night outs – spend some nights at home thinking about making more money
- Gambling – if you plan to gamble, it is better to gamble in a business
- Vacation and Country Clubs – you won't die without a few memberships
- Food – eat healthily and you can even think clearer
- Laziness – The biggest thing that will hold you back!

Most important of all, don't buy anything that constitutes a liability. A liability is anything that takes money out of your pocket no matter what they are worth in the future. Think in terms of cash flow. What can I invest in today that will give me funds tomorrow?

Now let's move on to offensive strategies:

Offensive Strategies

One of the best, low-cost ways to invest in your business skills is to join a Network Marketing company. There are many other options such as starting a traditional business or maybe even an Online Business. But if you want to guarantee yourself something concrete where business skills are concern, my take is on Network Marketing.

Regardless of what you have heard about this industry or how much money people have lost there, the biggest reason why I would recommend everyone to invest in a network marketing company is because of what you can learn there, and not because of how much money you can make (although it would be fantastic if you can make a living out of it). You see, network marketing companies are the one place where people will share their trade secrets FREELY. It is logical because in order for your up line to succeed, they will want you to succeed as well! Therefore, they will not hold back in teaching you the skills of a business person. Furthermore, the relatively low cost of investing in a network marketing company will amaze you for what you can learn for the price you are paying (a few bottles of vitamins and a business kit for the experience of a lifetime!) They will patiently train you in the attitudes and business skills you need to succeed in this industry. Basically, you can't succeed in network marketing with an employee's mindset.

A network marketing company will train you in sales, communication, teamwork, leadership, positive thinking, self-improvement, time and money investment as well as the support of your up line as a personal coach and mentor. I dare say that even if you didn't make a cent, but diligently went through their program, the skills you develop will last a lifetime. You can also develop skills by attaching yourself to an insurance agency. The job may be challenging, but those companies will also teach you the same skills above and maybe even gain a few tips on financial planning as well.

How about an Internet business? If you have the aptitude for computers, Internet businesses offer a low cost, high-profit margin business that can earn a lot of money and tap into a worldwide market. Other places you can learn about business skills can be found at financial planning courses, real estate investment courses, time management courses and lots more. All these I have suggested will be the safest way you can start a new business. You are only spending a few hundred to a thousand dollars in start-up and education.

A traditional business might be too risky for someone without any business experience. You invest tens of thousands of dollars and you might struggle trying to break even. But once you have developed the skills above, you will have a higher chance of succeeding. The most important things, besides a good learning attitude, are the people you mix around with. It has been said before; you are the sum of the five people you spend the most time with! This is very hard to swallow but imagine if you start talking to your five beer drinking, poker buddies that you want to go out on your own and make a fortune, what would they tell you? They would laugh their socks off before tearing your ego into a million pieces!

At the heart of man lies jealousy. They don't want to see the people around them succeed. If you succeed, it makes them look bad. They know in their hearts that they are going nowhere yet they embrace that lifestyle and pull you down with them. They will steal your dream, and rob you of your financial freedom if you are not careful!

The key point to remember is: Only mix with Positive thinking people! Positive thinking is not wishful thinking. A wishful thinker is a dreamer who doesn't take action. Positive thinking is backed by action and you will feel the energy of people who believe in you and support your dreams. If you hang out with ducks, you will quack... but if you hang out with eagles, you will soar! So start looking for people who will follow your vision or are willing to grow together with you.

Lastly, you must BELIEVE IN YOURSELF! The task of stepping out of your comfort zone may seem terrifying and many will not support your dream. They may even go on the offensive even if you don't share your dream. That person may even be your parents or your spouse. Then you will be faced with the question, is my financial freedom worth the price I am paying now? Can I live another day with the same routine, the same job, the same paycheck or the same drudgery? If the answer is no, then take action NOW. Not tomorrow, you will wake up and forget about your dream. Write down your desire on a piece of paper and hang on tight to it every day. Share it with someone positive and take that first step. You won't regret it.

ABOUT THE AUTHOR

Betty Wright works as a financial consultant to high net-worth families. Over the years, she has built a portfolio of successful businesses that were born from her interactions with her clients and the resulting pieces of business advice

www.ingramcontent.com/pod-product-compliance
Lightning Source LLC
Chambersburg PA
CBHW051254170526
45165CB00004B/1714